Stories of Children to Make You Smile

. . . an advertisement for birth control

Sandra Ludwick

BALBOA.PRESS

A DIVISION OF HAY HOUSE

Balboa Press books may be ordered through booksellers or by contacting:

Balboa Press
A Division of Hay House
1663 Liberty Drive
Bloomington, IN 47403
www.balboapress.com
844-682-1282

Because of the dynamic nature of the Internet, any web addresses or
links contained in this book may have changed since publication and
may no longer be valid. The views expressed in this work are solely those
of the author and do not necessarily reflect the views of the publisher,
and the publisher hereby disclaims any responsibility for them.

The author of this book does not dispense medical advice or prescribe the use
of any technique as a form of treatment for physical, emotional, or medical
problems without the advice of a physician, either directly or indirectly. The
intent of the author is only to offer information of a general nature to help
you in your quest for emotional and spiritual well-being. In the event you use
any of the information in this book for yourself, which is your constitutional
right, the author and the publisher assume no responsibility for your actions.

Any people depicted in stock imagery provided by Getty Images are
models, and such images are being used for illustrative purposes only.
Certain stock imagery © Getty Images.

Print information available on the last page.

ISBN: 978-1-9822-5531-2 (sc)
ISBN: 978-1-9822-5532-9 (e)

Balboa Press rev. date: 09/22/2020

DEDICATION

To the father of, and the children who have provided me with so much writing material.

CONTENTS

ACKNOWLEDGMENTS

First and foremost, I would like to say thank you to all my family and friends who have helped me along this journey. If it were not for their support, the stories in this book that I am sharing would be nothing but wonderful memories. This way, as I get older, and my memory fails, I can just pick up the book and know that I have lived these adventures. To Russ, and our three wonderful children, Michelynn, Nancie, and Brian, I say a special thank you for sharing our little adventures.

A special thank you also needs to go out to my father, who first encouraged me to do this. In reminding me of all the mishaps, he was right to believe that they would fill a book. And, these stories are only a sampling of a lifetime of events. A follow-up sequel will be forthcoming for adult adventures and calamities.

Lastly, I cannot even begin to thank my mentor, editor, and friend, Beverly Moss Haedrich. She has been my rock through this process and shared many insights with me. So, it was only natural that I share my adventures with her.

INTRODUCTION

Today we live in very troubling times. And, for that reason alone, we should have something positive to smile about. Thus, the stories contained herein are designed for just that purpose. These stories, however, are not unique. And, whether you are a parent, grandparent, another family member, or just someone who can relate to children, you may see yourself and others within these pages.

Many years ago, Art Linkletter, a talented interviewer, had a television program called *KIDS SAY THE DARNDEST THINGS*. You may remember it. A simple question answered by a child left the audience rolling in the isles. However, it has been my experience that kids not only say the darndest things; they do the darndest things. Hence, I dedicate these stories to the creativity and ingenuity of our younger generations, and those other individuals who tag along.

Let me also add that no one loves their children more than I do. The secondary title, ' . . . an argument for birth control,' is my attempt to relay the fact that sometimes, ignorance can be bliss! If we only knew what we were in for when we bring those little bundles into the world, we would probably say, "Send it back!" But somehow, the majority of them turn out to be productive citizens and the joy of our lives.

I invite you to read on as I share my joy with you.

The stories are grouped into chapters by subject. And, because most of us lead hectic lives, these are short tales allowing you the freedom to read as much or as little as you like at one sitting. The important take-away, if you will, is that in the midst of the current chaos, there is also beauty in the form of humor.

What we need to do is find and hold on to that humor to help us stay balanced. In sum, instead of focusing on the negative, let us emphasize the positive. And that, in itself, should give us reason to smile!

CHAPTER 1

BEHAVIOR

Most anyone who has spent any length of time around children could write an entire thesis on their behavior. However, that is not what this book is about. This book is about three children, who were raised in the same family, with the same rules, but who all turned out very differently. I am sure that you might find that same issue in your family. Whatever personality traits, environmental factors, or basic genetics they acquired made these little creatures into the individuals they have become today. Those factors have shaped their being.

And, let me say that this book is not about pointing out any flaws. It is about normal children doing everyday things. Our family journey is meant for entertainment and educational purposes only so that you may not make some of the same mistakes we did.

Family Ranking

Did you know that birth ranking of children in family matters? The oldest child, for instance, often displays personality traits of being a people pleaser, leader, and sometimes bossy or a know-it-all. They may even be controlling or attention-seeking.

On the other hand, the baby or youngest family member tends to be humorous and act out in silly or funny ways. He or she may also be friendly, creative, and idealistic. They may feel inferior, bore easily, be self-centered, and expect others to care for their needs.

Lastly, the middle child, however, tends to be more flexible and easy-going. These children are highly adaptable to situations and, therefore, often become the negotiators. These children also tend to be extremely competitive and determined.

Sometime before my son was born, I had been scheduled for a medical procedure, and my parents had agreed to watch the two girls. According to my mother, the girls proved to be too much for my dad. So, my husband and I picked the girls up earlier than originally planned. Apparently, the main issue was that daughter number two, being the independent one, refused to let my dad do anything for her. For example, as we were leaving, dad tried to help her with her coat. Turning around to face him, her comment was, "Pap-Pap, I can do it myself!"

Years later, I had the opportunity to watch this family ranking play out first-hand among the children. On one occasion, I had been unhappy with daughter number one, the oldest of the three children, and was somewhat scolding her. Several minutes later, I heard her turn to her younger sister, the middle child, and begin to scold her. Daughter number two then turned to my son, the youngest of the three, and did exactly what her sister had done to her. My son, looking around and rather stunned, began scolding the dog. The poor dog sat there, just cocking her head from side to side. She was the only one around with less ranking in the family than any of the others.

All the children stayed true to their family ranking traits throughout their childhood and into adulthood, and now they have children of their own who display some of these very same traits.

Imagine that!

The Dirt Bike

Have you ever heard of women's intuition? It is a sixth sense ingrained in the soul, especially when it comes to mothers and children. Over the years, there have been numerous documentations of such events. Very often, mothers have had this innate sense that something was wrong with one of their children, and they have been right. Well, my intuition came knocking on an ordinary, nondescript day.

My son was about twelve or thirteen at the time. That particular morning, while I was getting ready for work, he told me that he was not feeling very well. He rarely got sick, so I did not think much of it. He said that he had a headache and his stomach was upset. I checked to see if he had any fever, but he did not. I then ask him if he thought he should be going to school. We both agreed he should probably stay home that day and rest, and I went off to work.

I was at work, about 11:00 o'clock that morning, when one of those pangs of mother's intuition struck. I decided that I should go home at lunchtime and check on him. I wanted to make sure he was feeling okay. I left work about a half an hour later and began the drive home.

When I turned onto our street, I saw a police car. I wondered what that was all about. A few minutes later, I pulled into my driveway. As I got out of my car, I turned and looked down the street. I realized the policeman was talking to my son, who was on his dirt bike no less. I immediately marched myself down the sidewalk to where they were talking and asked what the devil was going on. The policeman asked who I was, and I identified myself as this boy's mother. The policeman said he had seen that my son was outside, and he was inquiring as to why the young man was not in school.

At that point, I intervened and assured the policeman that I would promptly take care of the matter. He took one look at me and had no doubt about what I was saying. It seemed he could not get in his patrol car fast enough, and I really think when he left, he felt sorry for my son. He obviously knew the signs of an angry mother.

Discipline, not any illness, soon followed.

CHAPTER 2

SCHOOL

S chool is more than a physical building. It is the process of education happening within and outside of the building that is the event. Education can happen in any place, any situation, or at any time. Education occurs from birth through the lifetime of an individual and takes many forms. It could be formal, home, or OJT (on the job training), as is the case with the following story.

Heads Up

There are similarities among family members that cannot be disputed. Some are genetic in nature, yet others are environmental. One particular story comes to mind that might fall into either category.

Being a graduate of the University of Delaware, my husband and I decided to attend one of their football games. Since this was a spur-of-the-moment decision, the only seats we could get were in the end zone. It was a beautiful sunny day, and the game was progressing well. Delaware had a particularly good team that year. Suddenly, everyone began to yell, "Heads up!" Not being a football expert, and following what everyone else was doing, I turned my head to the sky and began to look up. I had absolutely no idea why. All of a sudden, WHACK! The football hit me on the head.

Everything went black. I could hear, but I could not see anything. My husband grabbed my arm and was shaking me. I heard him say, "Are you all right?" I could not answer, but my brain was still at work. All I could think of was, 'how do you think I feel? I just got hit on the head with a football.' After a few minutes, the blackness began to disappear, and I regained my vision and speech. I now know what heads up means.

However, the story does not end there. A short time later, my husband attended the local high school football game. For some reason, I was not able to go that day. My husband had to leave the game early but called me on his way home. "I just heard on the radio that one of the cheerleaders got hit on the head with a football," he said. Our daughter number two was a high school cheerleader.

"For heaven sakes," I replied. "It is not genetic." About that moment, the front door opened, and you will never guess who it was. Right, daughter number two. She had been the one who got hit on the head with the football.

Now I ask you, "Genetics or environmental?"

CHAPTER 3

TRAVEL

"Are we there yet?" "I have to go to the bathroom!" "Johnny has his foot on my side of the car." Do any of these phrases sound familiar? Surely, if you have been on a trip with any children, you know what I am talking about. How often have you counted yellow cars, or perhaps cows in the field, or maybe even played the "punch buggy" game when you saw a VW?

The next three stories have to do with travel, but one may not be the trip you might expect.

The Runaway

It is not uncommon for children to reach into their little arsenal of tricks and pull out the "I am running away" card when they do not get their own way. However, there are those children who just talk about it and those children who do it. I have always stressed to my children that if they were that unhappy, and felt the need to leave home, let me know, and I would help them find a place to go. After all, there is no need to be stupid about the situation. And, there are many harmful things in that big, bad, imperfect world out there.

As a parent, I cannot tell you how terrifying it is to discover one of your children has run away. Utter panic does not even begin to describe the feeling. Well, that is just what happened in our household when daughter number two, at the age of sixteen, decided to leave. As time went by, and she did not return home, all sorts of horrible thoughts began to run through everyone's head. They were worst-case scenarios. They were thoughts so terrible that you dared not express them out loud.

My husband and I began calling everyone our daughter knew to try and get even a hint at where she might be. We knew the police would not act until she was missing for at least twenty-four hours. By that evening, however, we could not stand the waiting any longer and decided to call the police. They were extremely helpful and said they would keep us updated. No one slept much that night, and by late afternoon of the next day, she had been located. The police had asked if we wanted to get her or wanted them to bring her home. We opted for the latter, but not without reason.

It seems daughter number two and her girlfriend had decided that they needed a vacation from everything. The stress of school and parents was getting to them. However, they had taken at least some of my advice and were not stupid about the situation. The girls had planned it out very carefully. They had saved their money, gotten a motel room, and had enough food to last them during their little break.

They had never planned to stay away forever; they just needed a bit of a vacation.

Daughter number two was totally mortified when she was driven home in a police car. After all, an incident like that could have tarnished her stellar reputation.

Gratefully, a repeat incident never happened again.

The Castle

It was summer, and my father had arranged for him and a friend, my sister with husband and son, and me with husband, two daughters, and a son to have a vacation in Myrtle Beach, South Carolina. The facility was beautiful, complete with a pool and right on the ocean. We spent our days there, and everyone got together at around 4:00 pm to go out to dinner and do our activities.

One particular evening sticks in my mind as we had our usual dinner and then decided to walk on the boardwalk. We all had a picture taken together in costumes, while almost passing out from the heat. There was also a haunted house wax museum there that looked like an old Castle. On the outside, it seemed rather authentic. And they even had a person dressed as Frankenstein walking around out front. The attraction caught my eye immediately, and I thought the children would enjoy it. So off we went to get our tickets.

As we got closer, my son, approximately age five or six at that time, began to chant. "I don't want to go in there," he said. He began

13

to get louder each time he repeated his sentence. His father picked him up, and we both reassured him that everything would be fine. We got our tickets and went inside. The path we were to follow was barely lit.

Sighting the first display, my son began to switch his sentence to, "Get Me Out of here!" There was no changing his mind at this point, so his dad took him outside. There the two of them waited for the girls and me to come out. The girls loved it. But, for the rest of the night, all we heard from our son was, "I told you I didn't want to go in there," over and over again. People walking by would just smile or chuckle as they heard this little guy walking along, muttering rather loudly. In spite of it all, everyone had a great time, and it gave us all a chance to be together.

The Last Vacation

The summer that my oldest daughter graduated high school, we took a trip to West Palm Beach, Florida. It was the last family vacation we would take. As a single parent, I could hardly even afford a vacation, but we would be staying with friends, so the cost was minimal. All the children were getting older, and soon everyone would begin to go their separate ways.

The vacation itself was fantastic. However, the car broke down in St. Augustine, on the way home and the real adventure began. I was able to drive to a gas station where the gentleman said that the alternator had gone bad. Luckily, I had the car warranty in the glove box.

While we stood in 100 plus degree heat, daughter number two (age sixteen) announced that she had broken a nail. What a real crisis we had! I could not help but laugh as I realized our circumstances were dire and how my daughter detached herself from the situation.

The temperature kept getting warmer, and tempers began to get shorter as we continued to wait for the tow truck to pick us up and take us to a repair shop. After a while, daughter number two again announced: "Mom, I think I'll fly home. I really can't deal with all of this," she said very matter of fact. The irony is that daughter number two had always been the most determined, hard-working, and focused of my three children. Daughter number one followed by saying that she, too, was going to fly home. At which point, my son (the youngest of the three) spoke up with a "Me too!" I replied that unless he was paying his own way, he was stuck with me for the duration.

The tow truck finally arrived, and the driver could not have been more helpful. He took us to a safe but reasonable hotel for lodging on the way to drop the car off at the shop. I soon received a phone call from the shop that they would have to order the part. It was Saturday afternoon, and we would be stuck there until at least Wednesday.

After we checked into the hotel, the two girls got on the phone to make their arrangements for a trip back home. They even called for a shuttle to pick them up. They got their showers and just had time to finish before the shuttle arrived. Off they went.

The next day, the tow truck driver called and invited my son and me to his home for dinner and to see his new baby girl. He said there was a pool so we could swim, and it would help to pass the time. He would even come and pick us up. My son and I spent the day at his house and had a really wonderful time. We returned to the hotel that evening.

Fortunately, the car part arrived late Monday, and by Tuesday afternoon, my son and I were on our way back to Delaware. He slept most of the way, waking only briefly to ask if I wanted him to drive (even though he was under-age). I drove straight through, except to stop for combined gas and potty breaks. About twelve hours later, we were home again and what a relief it was.

You may think that this is the end of the story, but there is a moral to it. When I returned to work the following morning, I relayed our little adventure to my secretary. Her jaw dropped, stating that she thought it was awful that two of my children left me there. I told her that at first, I felt the same way, but then I thought about it. Even though I would never have left them in such a situation I realized they had done me a favor.

The thought of being stuck in a hotel room with two additional girls who did not want to be there was overwhelming. They both wanted to get home to see their boyfriends, would have been bored and would have been less than congenial in such a situation. They really, in essence, did me a favor because of their decision, relieving me of a lot of undue stress.

The moral you might ask is this. Our children do not really belong to us. They are given to us on loan so that we can teach them through lessons and examples to grow up and become independent, contributing, and responsible citizens. With that last thought in mind, I felt I had done my job. I now know that the girls are self-sufficient and able to take care of themselves. My son has yet to be determined.

CHAPTER 4

HEALTH

Most people would agree that nothing is more important than your health, be it physical or mental. Most children have a built-in activity switch that keeps them exercising from morning to night. I so envy them. For most parents and others interacting with those bundles of energy, it is hard to even keep up with them as a close second.

I would also suggest that there is a part of our mental health that is super important to everyone, whether they are big or little. And that is being able to keep our sense of humor. We have to learn and teach our children to see the humor in situations and be able to laugh at ourselves from time to time. For humor may truly be the best medicine of all.

Ballet Gloves

There is nothing better for health than exercise. Even though children have their own "on switch" for constant movement, dancing gives them a structured environment in which to participate. As I remember, it was not a particularly good morning to begin with. The weekend fun had passed, and it was Monday, i.e., washday at my house. I had been struggling with the children to clean up their rooms. Let's just say that they were less than enthused for the task at hand.

When I began sorting the clothing for the different wash loads, I noticed a pair of dancing gloves in the hamper. The gloves belonged to the costumes the girls had just worn in a recital the Friday before. "Who put the dancing gloves in the hamper?" I asked.

Now, you already know how this is going to go. "I didn't do it," said daughter number one. "Well, I didn't do it," said daughter number two. "Oh," I said. "So, the gloves just jumped in there all by themselves." Needless to say, things escalated and neither girl would own up. From my perspective, it was not the gloves in the hamper that was the issue. It was the fact that one of the girls was not telling the truth. The end result was that each girl had to stand facing a corner of the dining room until someone confessed to the crime.

I think it was worse for me than it was for the girls, but no one was talking. I really cannot remember how much time passed, but it seemed like forever. Finally, daughter number two broke down and said, "Well, I'll say I did it just to get out of this stupid corner, but I really didn't do it." I had to turn my head to keep from chuckling.

I wanted to know who really committed the crime, so to speak, so the girls remained in the corner a little while longer. Finally, I broke and let them out.

Today they are married with children and grandchildren of their own. And do you know what? I still do not know who put the gloves in the hamper. Recently, I have seen a new commercial on television. The theme is centered around "I didn't do it."

Now, I ask you, are they talking about my children or yours?

A Curbside Tale

The month was March, but it was warm as I remember. My husband and I were leaving for a trip to New York City that afternoon. Our oldest daughter, about six or seven years old at the time, was in a class on that Saturday morning, and I had gone to pick her up.

Walking to the car, daughter number one missed the curb and went down on her knee. I do not, to this day, understand how she could have done so much damage. The knee was bleeding profusely, so I took her back into the building to clean her up. As usually happens, everyone came running over, offering suggestion after suggestion. Finally, I said that I was taking her to the Emergency Room to get her checked out. I could see tiny, finely ground stones in the wound, and I did not want her to get an infection.

After we arrived at the Emergency Room, I was trying to keep her calm. Even at a young age, she was quite the little actress, and I did not want her to get hysterical. She was doing fine, but then they took her away from me. I had to stay and fill out paperwork. There I sat, my hair in curlers, trying to keep an ear toward the double swinging doors where they took my daughter. I became aware that I told them the wrong birth date when the registrar asked, "She's 76?" Obviously, my concentration was understandably elsewhere. They finally let me go back to her.

We were in a surgical room when the doctor came in to examine her. It went without saying that she would need stitches. About that time, a nurse came through one of the doors. The doctor said, "I asked for a surgical nurse forty-five minutes ago." The nurse replied, "You know how it is around here at lunchtime, doc," and went out the other door.

The doctor then looked at me and said, "Are you going to be all right?" I replied with a nod and simply said, "Yes." The doctor began his work. My only concern was keeping my daughter calm and still. Everything went well and we returned home. But you know, in our household things were never simple, and this event was no exception. Within a week, our daughter had fallen down the stairs and busted all the stitches open.

This swan dance of busting the knee open again and again went on from the beginning of March into July. Finally, I had had enough. I went into the garage, found a piece of 2x4 inch wood, and taped it to her leg. It certainly did not stop her from being too rambunctious, but it slowed her down considerably.

We returned to the doctor in August. The wound had finally closed, but a big lump had formed. I had to soak her knee every four hours. Right before school started, the doctor finally cleared her from his care. He recommended plastic surgery, but I replied, "What child doesn't have a scar on their knee? When she grows up and gets a job, she can pay for the plastic surgery if she still wants it.

I was done!

Catastrophes

If you have more than one child, I am sure you can relate to the fact that one is usually clumsier than the others. That was certainly the case in our family. For the most part, it was daughter number two who was the clumsy one. However, she never seemed to get hurt by her acts of contortion. The other two children were almost tied for the championship. But I think the real winner was my son.

It all began when he was small, probably about three years old. He was sleeping in his youth bed. My husband and I were watching television, and suddenly we heard a thump. We looked at each other and then ran to check on the children. Sure enough, my son had fallen out of bed and broken his collarbone. So off to the Emergency Room we went. The bed was barely a foot off the ground, but I guess it is all in how you land. It was summer, hot and I could not keep my son out of the pool. He wanted to join his sisters. So, every nap time and bedtime, I would run his collar brace through the dryer for the next go-round.

A few years later, the next significant issue occurred. I had just come home from the hospital that day. I had pre-planned a Brownie event with three troops of girls that my co-leader was going to handle. My oldest daughter walked to the school and returned home crying. The school was all locked up, and she thought it was her fault for not reminding the janitor to open the door. I got her settled and told my husband to start moving furniture. We were going to have sixty plus Brownies in our living room. About halfway through, my co-leader called and said the school had been opened. My husband left in the van to take my daughter back up to the school, taking my son with him. I headed to bed.

Now, you might ask what this has to do with my son's catastrophes. Well, backing out of the driveway in the van, my son fell forward and busted his lip open. Seatbelts were not a requirement then. My husband came back in the house with my son's mouth bleeding everywhere. I knew he would need stitches. So, while my husband took my daughter back up to school, I called my neighbor over to go to the hospital with my husband and son. I was not allowed to ride in the car because of my recent back surgery. Disaster resolved, I returned to the bed a second time.

Not but a few minutes later, I heard the front door open and someone called. It was my sister-in-law and her husband. They lived miles from us and seldom came to visit, except on holidays. However, they were in the area that day and decided to stop in. I am sure they were shocked coming in and seeing the house all torn up. Half of the living room furniture had been pushed to a corner. My sister-in-law asked where her brother was, and I told her he was on the way to the hospital with our son. She replied, "What else is new?" and just laughed.

My son had always been a rather cautious child. You would not necessarily call him a thrill seeker. However, these little accidents continued throughout his youth and into his young adult years. Probably the most significant was when he had a close encounter with another ballplayer. He was about seventeen or eighteen, and a member of the Volunteer Fire company with his dad.

It was a summer afternoon when I received the call from the hospital telling me my son was there. Of course, I went right over. When I arrived, the staff was in the middle of stitching his cheek back together. The impact between the players was so great that my son's skin actually ruptured. The accident had also moved his cheekbone from where it should have been to his temple area. He had broken his eye socket in three places. They would have to do surgery as soon as they could get it scheduled.

I only had one question for him. "So, what does the other guy look like?" I asked. Fortunately, everything turned out fine, but his sinuses still suffer from the incident. It seems that my son and the other ballplayer were both going after the same ball. The close encounter was between my son's cheek and the other guy's jaw.

However, the story continues. As my son got older, he was involved in a three-car accident. It seems he was the middle of the sandwich. Several back operations later, he seems to be doing quite well, and the rest of us hold our breath that the incident was the last of the major catastrophes.

As the song says, "What doesn't kill you makes you stronger."

Lights Out

I don't know about you, but I can stomach just about anything from broken or severed body parts, gashes and such. But, one of the first things I taught my children was that if they were going to be sick, they better make it to the bathroom. I am just not good at cleaning up vomit, even my own!

One particular evening I had agreed to watch my friend's two boys while she attended a meeting. The boys were the same ages as my two girls, and they all went to the same school. So, they knew each other very well.

Shortly after the boys were dropped off at my house, the sky became very dark, and the heavens began to open up, if you know what I mean. It poured rain like you have never seen. The lightning and thunder were so loud it echoed through the house. And, there I was by myself, with five children all under the age of seven. Suddenly, the electricity went off. I looked out of the window, and everyone's lights were out for as far as I could see.

What's next? I thought to myself, and I quickly came up with an alternate plan for the evening. I told the children we were going to have an inside picnic and ask them if they had ever done that before. They all said, "No." So I grabbed a flashlight and set about gathering supplies. The first thing I did was to get extra flashlights to pass around, and I pulled a large blanket from the linen closet. I spread the blanket out on the living room floor and got all the children situated on it.

Next, I headed to the kitchen to get snacks and drinks for all of the children. You cannot have a picnic without food! And, as I told the children, the best part of an indoor picnic was that you do not have any ants to bother you. Well, everything was going fine. We all sang songs and told stories until . . .

My son, the youngest of the group and almost two years old, began to get sick and throw up. I was cleaning that up when one of my daughters announced she was not feeling well herself. Just as I sent her to the bathroom, the front door opened. It was my friend returning. With all the lights out due to the storm, the meeting was canceled.

My friend gathered up her two boys saying their goodbyes and wishing us good luck. However, living a short distance from me, it was not long before she called. She and the boys had made it home and almost into the house when one of the boys began getting sick at the bottom of the stairs. Go figure! At least they were outside, and it was raining to wash things off.

Like I have always said, children of that age should be referred to as 'baby incubators.'

Oh, My Aching Back

Have you ever used the phrase: "If Johnny (or someone else) jumped off a bridge, would you do it?" I know that I have said those words to my children many times, until one day . . .

I received a phone call from the hospital Emergency Room. The caller had identified herself and told me that my oldest daughter was there. I hung up the phone and immediately headed straight to the hospital. As I arrived, my daughter's boyfriend was waiting at the entrance to fill me in on the details. That day, my daughter and her boyfriend had been together with another couple on a picnic.

It was early March and a beautiful spring-like day. They had all gone to a wooded park to enjoy the outdoors and the nice weather.

As the boyfriend explained, the guys were jumping off an old railroad bridge into a sandpit below. At some point my daughter decided, in the wisdom of her youth, that if the guys could do it, so could she. The problem was not, however, in the jumping, but in the landing. Well, my daughter landed alright, but had a problem when she tried to get up.

The guys called for help. The emergency crew had planned to airlift my daughter, but the helicopter could not land because of the trees. Thus, when the ambulance arrived, they transported her to the hospital.

The doctor was exceptional. He cautiously took his time reading the x-rays and other case studies. He consulted with other doctors and me to develop the best possible plan of care. After discussions were completed, the decision was made to do surgery. The only other option was to keep her lying stable for six months. I explained to the doctor how that would never work with this child.

The problem: no one knew for sure if she would ever walk again. It took three surgeons twelve hours of surgery, and a set of metal rods, to mend her broken back.

I spent many weeks working half the day in my office and half in the hospital until my daughter could return home. Thankfully, the back surgery was successful. However, being the active child that she had always been, she worked the rods loose until they rolled across her back and had to be removed several years later.

She is now an adult and has her own children to take care of and look after. The great news is her back is fine. But I have never asked the jumping off the bridge question again. I had my answer.

CHAPTER 5

CHRISTMAS

C hristmas, in the secular sense, is about fun and festivities, especially for most children. Ask any teacher or parent how overly excited the children are around any holiday, but especially Christmas, and you will not be surprised at the answer. They are overwhelmed with anticipation.

However, sometimes the holiday does not turn out exactly as we have planned. The following stories are not typical in the sense of bliss, bliss, bliss. But they do reveal an underlying moral.

A True Christmas Story

Most everyone knows **THE CHRISTMAS STORY** about a little boy who desperately wanted nothing but a Red Rider gun for his Christmas present. His parents and teacher told him repeatedly that he would shoot his eye out. This made-for-TV story may be fictional, but I can tell you a true Christmas story involving another little boy, my son.

Some years ago, as the Christmas holiday was getting closer and the schools had not let out yet, we had an incident. And in one rather ordinary morning after sending my children off to school, I received a phone call from the school nurse.

"Mrs. Smith," the nurse said. "I have your son in my office." Now I can tell you that many things ran through my mind at that moment. Is my child hurt? Has my child been in an accident? Is my child ill, bleeding or in a comma? "What is the problem?" I asked with a calm but hesitant tone in my voice. I postured myself for the news. "It seems that your son stuck his tongue to a metal lamp post outside, and the bus driver had to pry him off," the nurse replied. I knew immediately what had taken place.

You see, the night before, we as a family had watched **The Christmas Story** movie on television. Apparently, my nine-year-old son did not believe the movie, so he decided to test out the incident himself. "Should I be concerned?" I asked the nurse. She replied, "Just watch out for infection."

Later that afternoon, as I heard the front door open as my son came home from school, I called out, "I am down here." I was downstairs in the family room. My son began to descend the steps . . . thump, thump, thump.

I said, "Just tell me one thing. Was it a triple-dog-dare?" In a very muffled and tongue-tied manner, he replied, "I *dhon't whant* to *thalk* about it."

This is one stunt my son would never live down. Through the years he has taken grief from me, his dad, and his two older sisters over the incident. We have showered him with a copy of the movie and all sorts of other memorabilia. He is now a grown man, but the tradition continues. Thank goodness he has been a good sport about it all.

Last Christmas, while shopping, I spied a Red Rider gun. Now you know that I just had to get it. I wrapped it carefully and attached a note in bold print that read, "Don't shoot your eye out!"

The Coupon

If you have, or had more than one child, you already know how different each one of them can be. These differences may involve genetics, environment as well as birth ranking within the family (as discussed in the Family Ranking story).

In our family, daughter number two was the classic middle child. She was incredibly independent yet responsible. She worked hard in school and at her job and prepared for just about any situation. However, she appreciated 'labels' and the other finer things in life.

If, for example, we went shopping, daughter number one and my son would be happy with anything they got. Daughter number two, on the other hand, was much more selective. If she could not find what she wanted, she would just not get anything at all and wait until another time. Or, she would save her own money until she could get what she wanted. Because she was so responsible, it was difficult not to honor her choices.

However, every parent waits for those rare opportunities when they can have some fun. That was the case before Christmas one year. I happened to be browsing through the paper, and I came across one of those discount store ads. Now, I personally am always looking for where I can get the best price on what I want, be it a discount store or a top-notch store that is having a great sale. I always ask myself, "How much am I willing to pay for this item?" Or, "Do I want the item badly enough to pay X number of dollars for it?"

Anyway, I could not resist the opportunity presented and grabbed my scissors. I cut out the ad, not for myself, but for daughter number two. I took the ad and wrote a note, 'We got you a gift certificate for Christmas,' and taped it to her bedroom door. Then, I patiently waited for her to come home from school. I knew I would be aware the minute the ad caught her eye. It was not long before I heard her footsteps in the hallway. "Hello," I said. "Hi," was her reply.

It was not but a few seconds when I heard the sound of paper tearing. I counted silently . . . one, two, three. "That wasn't funny!" said she emphatically.

Score one for mom's team!

Dragon Lady

Few times in my life had the Dragon Lady reared her ugly persona. However, one time before Christmas some years ago, she was summoned.

Sometimes life gets in our way and prevents us from doing scheduled activities. That is exactly what happened prior to that particular Christmas holiday. I had been sick with some type of flu bug, but I still had shopping to do. Children in tow, I headed off to the mall to fulfill my gift-giving responsibilities.

I promptly finished my shopping and made my way to the counter, where an obnoxious man had begun yelling. As could be expected, a clerk waited on him right away just to get him out of the store and on his way. 'Nothing like rewarding bad behavior,' I must have thought. Still feeling quite ill, I asked the clerk if there was a line; because I thought I was in it. Feeling sicker by the minute from the heat, my eyes glazed over, and Dragon Lady appeared.

The children all knew 'the look.' They very quickly excused themselves and said they would wait for me outside of the store in the center of the mall. Dragon Lady, rearing her ugly side, then looked at the clerk and said, "If you don't wait on me soon, I am going to throw up all over your counter!" There was no mistaking the truth of what this Dragon Lady was saying by the ashen color of her face.

Shortly after that, packages in hand, I left the store, gathered the children, and we all headed home for the holiday.

Goodbye, Dragon Lady!

Grandma Tears

The holidays are so special and such fun. However, there is also a certain amount of stress that can accompany the festivities. My best friend and I always joked about our annual Christmas cry when our children were young. For us, after the company was gone, the food put away, the dishes done, and the children safely in their beds, the exhaustion inevitably set in. It was at that vulnerable moment that the Christmas cry would happen.

I remember one Christmas in particular. I think there were about nineteen friends and family members at our house that day. Over time, I had gotten somewhat wiser and changed from a sit-down dinner with china to a self-serve buffet on paper plates. Mother almost disowned me but soon realized how much smoother things went. And I actually got to enjoy the company rather than being stuck running back and forth to the kitchen.

Anyway, that particular Christmas, I was busy trying to keep nineteen individuals fed, entertained, and happy. The children had been delighted with their gifts but became impatient as the day wore on. The older daughter had received a doll-making kit. Throughout the day, daughter number one kept asking to make her doll. It was not like that was the only toy she had to play with. I told her to be patient, and when the company left, I would help her make the doll. Among her other toys, the second younger daughter received a new doll to play with.

As the company began to leave, I noticed the children were unusually quiet. That was never a good sign. So, I went to check on them and discovered what I had feared. Daughter number one had worked on her doll kit, painting the face purple, and making other non-human adjustments. Daughter number two had given her new doll a haircut. Try to imagine a haircut given by a five-year-old. Some of the scalp was showing.

Needless to say, being exhausted, I did not react very well. I packed up all the Christmas gifts and put them in the attic. The children were then sent to bed. I told them if they were good, they could get two presents down each week.

After the dust settled, I went into the recreation room where the Christmas tree stood, and I prepared to have my annual Christmas cry by the lights of the tree. However, my plans soon changed when

I found my mother-in-law there . . .in tears. I asked her what was wrong. "I know they are your children, and you have to do what you think is best," she sobbed. "But they are only children," she added. I tried to remain calm as I explained, "Mom, your son had to work hard for the money to buy those gifts that the children just destroyed because they did not have the patience to wait."

The result: I think it was almost Easter when the last of the presents came down. And that was only because I could not stand to drag it out any longer. It was a hard lesson for all of us to learn.

CHAPTER 6

BIRTHDAYS

Most individuals like to celebrate birthdays. That is especially true if you are a child. Whether your child celebrates his or her birthday at school with classmates, at a designated party place, or just at home with family and friends, it can be a special day for anyone.

The Party

Each family has its own customs when it comes to birthday celebrations. Some individuals choose to spend their birthday quietly, while others opt for a big celebration. Our family usually tried to do something special for our children's birthdays each year.

If I remember correctly, I think it was the eighth birthday of daughter number two. Her dad and I had asked her how she would like to celebrate. She opted for a pizza party with her friends at the local pizza hang out. All the arrangements had been set ahead of time, and the day finally arrived. Everyone was to meet at the pizza place.

Since we had two other children, we told them they could each bring a friend. In addition, some of the invitees had younger and older siblings, so we also invited them. We ended up with a hodgepodge of children from about three to thirteen. I think we had about fifteen children there. Most of the parents dropped their children off and left. Together, the children, with varying heights, all looked like a staircase.

My husband and I sat at a strategically located booth, where we could keep an eye on everyone. The restaurant was mostly empty at that time of day. A short while later, a young couple entered the restaurant, looked around, and then came over and sat in the adjoining side booth by my husband and me. The couple was also watching the festivities and the children at the party. They seemed very friendly and said hello. We engaged in some light conversation.

My husband and I tried awfully hard not to intervene in our daughter's party. We wanted to let her be in charge, so to speak of her own party. The couple watched the excitement of the children playing, and after talking to them awhile, the young man commented, "You two must have a lot of fun at your house." We chuckled, looking at one another, and then I said, "Oh, we do! But we can't take credit for all of them." The couple sat stunned and then broke out in laughter.

A Surprise

Once in a great while, parents get a chance to slightly balance the score with their children. The time finally came when this opportunity presented itself to me with my son. It was my son's eighteenth birthday. I decided that particular age was sort of a rite of passage, so the celebration should be something special.

I made the arrangements for our evening of fun without telling my son. I called a couple of friends who were to go with us. My son had no idea where we were going until we pulled into the parking lot. There it was, in all of its orange glory, 'HOOTERS.' We went inside and ordered our dinners. My son thought that just going there was the surprise. No way! When I went to the lady's room to wash my hands, I came out of the restroom, and while my son was not looking, I made arrangements with some of the waitresses.

After we finished our dinner, it was time for us to order dessert. Everyone had their choice of what they wanted. My unsuspecting son ordered cheesecake. Now, I am sure that he was afraid that I would try and embarrass him with a birthday cake and candles in the middle of a restaurant. When the waitress came over to the table to serve the desert, she was joined by several other waitresses. They were all singing, 'Happy Birthday!'

My son's eyes got bigger, and his face got redder by the minute. He tried so hard to keep a cool, relaxed look on his face, that he was all but breaking out in a sweat. After the song finished, the waitresses shook glasses filled with silverware. If there was anyone in the restaurant who had not looked over during the song, they surely looked over at the noise. It was certainly a birthday to remember.

CHAPTER 7

PETS

What a beautiful creature! Magnificent, majestic, and mysterious are the three words that come to mind when describing this agile animal. Large or small, short or somewhat tall, the only thing for certain about this animal is that you will never know what it is thinking.

Covered with fur from its head to its tail, spotted or striped, solid or multicolored, long or short hair, the color diversity never ends. This animal has the sharpest of senses with ears that can hear over long distances. Its eyes become sharper as the day turns to night. Its nose can detect the keenest of smells. And, its whiskers can navigate the smallest of spaces. Some of the species have been known to travel up to twenty miles per night or run sixty to seventy-five miles an hour.

Evolving approximately fifteen million years ago in more fertile lands, this animal is associated with rebirth and resurrection. It is considered sacred, exalted, and intelligent. Known for its agility, tricks, and nine lives, it has been called Bastet by ancient Egyptians.

Do you know who I am? MEOW!

Sam

Many households have pets. Some households have just one pet, others have many. Throughout the years, in our household, I think we fell into the latter category. Before the children even came along, we began with a Siamese cat named Sam. Of course, he needed a friend, so a short while later we acquired another Siamese named Samantha.

While Samantha retained her thin and petite shape, Sam grew into quite the 'Tom.' What I remember most about him was when he flushed himself down the toilet. My husband and I were sitting on the sofa watching television, and we heard the toilet flush. We looked at each other, and before we had time to react, a wet streak flew passed us. All we could think was Sam must have walked across the back of the toilet, slipped, and caught his front paws on the handle going down. Water went everywhere, and he could not get out of there fast enough.

When our first child was born, Sam would guard her crib by lying across the doorway. My mother came to help me during that time. Every night she would trip over Sam on her way to get the baby. As our daughter grew, I watched when she tried to put a bonnet on the cat. Sam would sit there very patiently and let her. They seemed to have a special bond. I would see our now two-year-old pull that cat around by the tail. And, once I even saw them sharing a meal of cat food. Believe me, that was never intended.

Sam often played with his companion Samantha while our daughter was napping or otherwise occupied. Sam was a good old boy and was especially connected to our daughter. What a companion he was.

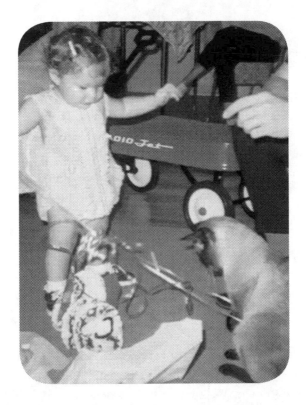

It's In The Water

One day, when the children were in their teenage years, my husband called from work and asked me if we would like to have a Labrador puppy. Someone he worked with had a dog that just had a litter, and he was trying to find good homes for the puppies. I said sure, the children would love it.

Well, when he brought the puppy home, she was so small she would fit in the palm of your hand. So, we named her Buttons because she was no bigger than one. She may have been born the runt of the litter, but she soon grew up to be more than an ample sized dog. Just in case you are not aware, labs mentally stay puppies for about two years. It is only after that time that they begin to settle down.

I distinctly remember Christmas times when we tried to coax Buttons away from the tree. Buttons never bothered the tree at all, but sometimes she got too close. That, in itself, was not a problem. However, when she got excited, her notoriously strong tail would wag. So, we would quietly call her name to coax her away from the tree, but her tail would begin to wag, and balls would drop and bounce off the walls and everywhere else. She just could not help herself.

After Buttons became an adult dog, our neighbors acquired a Beagle. They had gotten the Beagle, not for themselves, but because the original owner's wife had a baby and said the dog had to go. My neighbor could not keep the Beagle because he already had three dogs of his own. Every day I saw this Beagle by the fence with her big brown eyes, and my heart would just melt. Needless to say, the Beagle moved from next door to our house.

Strangely, almost every fall during hunting season, someone would steal her from our backyard. But somehow, by season's end, she would always find her way back home.

Now you might ask what these dogs have in common. And the answer is absolutely nothing, except for the puppies. The Beagle, who unknown to us was already pregnant, ended up having eleven puppies. That is almost unheard of for a Beagle. The Lab, not to be outdone by a Beagle, ended up having thirteen puppies!

It seemed that everyone in our house would multiply. Later we had three cats that all had litters within twenty-four hours of each other. We ended up with twenty-one kittens. The only thing I could do was to contain them in one area. When one of the mothers jumped in, all the kittens raced for a faucet.

Even our third child was unexpected. He always says he was a mistake, but I always say he was a miracle. It did seem that everything at our house multiplied. My friends would always joke about not drinking the water. For, after all, you could end up fertilized.

Pets And Critters Everywhere

Every Girl Scout Leader who is planning a camping trip must begin with essential 'survival' skills. These skills include, but are not limited to, adequate training, preparation for every imaginable emergency, a dose of fantastic planning, a group of girls that are so well behaved that they do not need a leader, a few talented co-leaders, and other suggestions thrown in from well-meaning 'friends.' One such suggestion was made to a Junior Leader in the New Castle area.

It is common knowledge that camping can be quite challenging for those beginning Junior girls who have had no camping experience. Naturally, you want to make them feel as comfortable as possible in strange surroundings. To help with this problem, it was suggested to the leader of the Troop that she encourage the girls to bring a bed 'pet' (stuffed animal) with them camping to help them feel more secure. And, with everyone bringing a 'pet,' no one would feel out of place or different.

Being flexible, another survival skill, the Leader welcomed this suggestion, and decided to have a 'pet' parade Saturday evening. The adult co-leaders even participated in the parade with their own animals. It turned out to be a fantastic weekend in spite of the rain.

The only problem that arose was somewhere between getting the girls nestled all snug in their beds, and before the visions of sugarplums could dance in their heads, the usual crises arose. Foreign visitors appeared on the scene. Some were brown wearing black masks to hide themselves, others were black with a white stripe down their back.

It was about the time that the first garbage can started to rattle that two 'buddies,' accompanied by a teddy bear, appeared in the troop house to gain the attention of their Leaders. "Mrs. Smith, Mrs. Smith," they exclaimed! "My teddy bear has smores stuck to his chin. I thought it was tar, but it smelled like marshmallows!" said she.

The moral of the story? If you are taking your bears to camp with you, do not let them get smores on their chin, or you may end up with more 'critters' than you bargained for.

CHAPTER 8

MISCELLANY

What can you say about "miscellany?" Not everything fits precisely into a tiny little box. So, the following stories are a hodge-podge collection of thoughts that I wanted to share. I think many of you can relate to, understand, or appreciate their intent.

Michelangelo

Let me just ask: "Have any of you ever had trouble explaining the concept of crayons, for example, to your children?" Well, let me tell you, those crayons were an obstacle that I thought would never be conquered at our house. I think it was partly my fault because I am a creative person. Before my son was born, I painted nursery rhymes on one of the walls, with Mother Goose in the center. How clever was that?

Now, you would not think that your children, about three and four at the time, pay any attention to you at all, but they really do. At the time of my well-intended effort, the girls never uttered one word, but little by little things began appearing in full 'colormatography.'

At first, there were little things like new faces on their dolls that suddenly appeared. Then, other things like walls had added color, and anything that did not move, including my toilet seat, begin to be in color. It seemed impossible to break them of this habit.

I was the only parent who went to their children's school conference and stated that her children were not allowed to use crayons in their home. My mother always thought it was funny until the girls stayed there one night and colored her bedsheets. Yes, I would say that I had a couple of Michelangelo's in the house. I guess I should blame myself for stifling their creativity. They might have been famous by now. Oh well . . .

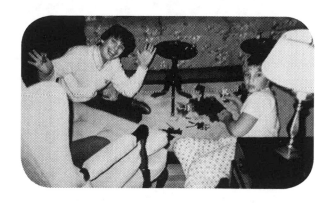

Sleeping Beauty

This is just a short story, but one I think is worth telling. While I had three children running around, and my house was usually in chaos, my sister only had one child. For the sake of argument, why not call him Robert. Being an only child, Robert was surrounded by adults and did not really have a chance to become just a kid.

My sister and I lived many miles and many states apart, so we did not get to visit very often.

I remember one visit in particular where Robert and my son, who were close in age, had themselves a grand old time. You see, my son was the youngest of three, and so he did not have much of a chance to retaliate against his two older sisters. However, with Robert there to help him, it was game on!

That particular morning, my oldest daughter liked to sleep late and was still in bed. Being a typical teenager, she liked to sleep late.

The boys were off supposedly playing somewhere, but I was not quite sure where. I noticed that it had gotten quiet. That was never a good sign, and moms have an uncanny way of tapping into quietness. I was just about to go check on the boys, when we all heard the blood-curdling scream. It had come from my daughter's room and could have woken the dead.

Without hesitation, I ran to her room only to find her tied to the bed. Apparently, the boys had been busy tying her up while she was sleeping and were now laughing hysterically. Sleeping Beauty, on the other hand, did not see the humor of the situation and was about to give them a lesson they would not forget . . . if she could only get untied.

Needless to say, I had to intervene in the situation. But I can tell you one thing. Robert had the time of his life just being a kid. And I am sure the incident made a memory he will never forget.

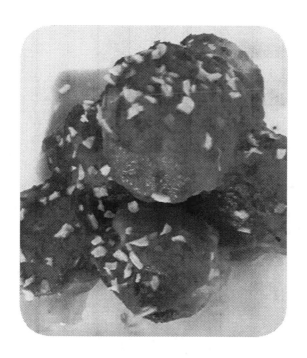

Meatballs

I had just returned home from the hospital after having back surgery. Getting settled in my own bed, I began planning the upcoming household duties that would need to be done.

In order to make things easier for my husband over the upcoming week, I was focused on creating a grocery list to help him. I suggested that he go to the store and buy five pounds of ground beef so that I could prepare burgers, a meatloaf, and meatballs to simplify mealtimes.

When my husband returned from the store, I got up, prepared the meatloaf, and then returned to the bed to rest. Next came the meatballs that I thought the children could handle making. They all shared an interest in cooking from an early age.

After resting for a short time, I again got out of bed and went to the kitchen to prepare the meatball mix. The oldest daughter was out, but I ask the other two children to roll the meatballs and place them in the oven at 350 degrees. Hindsight led me to believe I was not quite specific enough in my instructions. Not long after, I began to smell smoke.

For the third time that afternoon, I made my way to the kitchen. As I got closer, the smoke got thicker, and I began seeing a cloud of grey haze. Reaching the kitchen, I immediately spotted the source. The oven was on fire. I ran to the stove, and turned off the oven, and yelled at the youngest child to get out of the house. The next step was to dial 911 for the fire department.

You never know what you will do in an emergency until it actually happens. But on that day, I had my answer. The most insane words of wisdom that I will never forget came rolling out of my mouth. I said to my daughter who was still in the house with me, "Quick, take out the garbage. The firemen are coming." Now what can you possibly say after that?

But the story does not end here. You see, the true irony of the situation was that my husband was a volunteer fireman. So naturally when the firemen arrived at the house, they asked why my husband was not home fighting his own fires. Everyone had a good laugh over that one. But the truth of the matter was that I was scared to death my husband would hear that his house was on fire over his portable fire radio. As it turned out, he had gotten called to a traffic accident because he was primarily an EMT (Emergency Medical Technician).

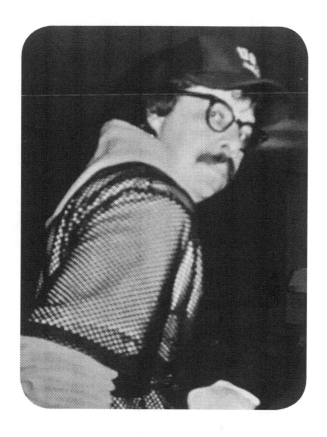

And, about the cause of the fire? My little darlings got tired. They decided to make the meatballs the size of softballs and put them in a broiler pan. Obviously, the grease overflowed the pan, and the fire began.

The good news was that nothing was damaged. And after airing the house out all afternoon, when my husband finally returned home, everything appeared to be normal. And, the garbage had been taken out!

Brownies

Brownies are my favorite people. And, I am not talking about the edible chocolate ones that you eat. Of all the years I spent in scouting; as a Brownie, as a Girl Scout, as a Leader, as a Consultant, and as an Area Chair, no one can compare to a Brownie. These first, second, and third-grade girls have both honesty and innocence and have created some of the best times in my life.

I remember one particular night that the troop was having some kind of ceremony. One of the little girls came to me, all upset. She tugged at the bottom of my jacket and said her parents were not coming because they had to go with her brother to the SPCA. I am quite sure she was referring to the school PTA (Parent Teacher Association).

Another time I remember putting thirty brownies on a bus with all their gear and some co-leaders of the troop and sending them camping. The bus got lost. Can you imagine explaining to thirty sets of parents why you do not know where their children are? An hour later, the bus finally showed up.

I also remember teaching the girls about classical music, taking them to their first ballet, and taking them to visit a nursing home. At the time, I was not sure how that would work out, but the girls were great. From then on, the nursing home would call me numerous times a year to bring the girls over. The residents and staff loved them and even gave them an Easter Egg Hunt at the facility.

I always tried to provide the girls with experiences they would not get elsewhere. For example, they had a stage debut in the play **Alice in Wonderland**. The school principal saw us practicing and asked me if we could perform the play for a school assembly. We ended up performing three assemblies. Even though the Rabbit got his umbrella caught in the Caterpillar's tail and spilled the 'drink me' water backstage, the girls were unscathed and acted like pros. For many of those girls, it would be the only time in their life they would be on a stage. The parents were wonderful and even helped to make the costumes.

However, one of the funniest incidents that really sticks out for me was when I sent an entire Brownie troop home with their clothes on backwards. I had decided that the girls needed some motivation.

I called the co-leaders and told them about the meeting's program. They were to wear their clothes backwards, and when the girls came in, they were to tell them goodnight and send them to the bathroom to switch their clothes around. We finished the evening with the opening ceremony. Now, would you believe I sent thirty girls home with their clothes on backwards and not one parent called to ask me why?

These girls and their experiences are some of my fondest memories. I still have a few pieces of their artwork from camping trips and other outings I have saved over the years. And whenever I see a Brownie, you know that I have to speak to her. After all:

**Make new friends,
But keep the old,
One is silver,
And the other gold.**

(A Brownie / Girl Scout song)

CONCLUSION

In conclusion, this book is about my reflections, i.e., special unforgettable moments and memories that I have carried with me on my journey through life. Often, we cannot appreciate those moments when they happen, but as we grow and our seasons change, their beauty grows upon us.

My hope is that each of you appreciates the special moments on these pages and in your own lives. And that you may find the humor in your surroundings, giving you a reason to smile each and every day.

"Oh, and the children?" you might ask. They have all grown up to be productive, successful citizens . . . in spite of their parents.

A NOTE:

I n all fairness to my children, I asked them to read this document before it went to the presses. I wanted to make sure that they were feeling alright about me reveling some of the stories I felt sure they would like to forget. They are now old enough to appreciate how sharing these stories could bring humor, or maybe even a teaching moment to others. I could not be prouder that they were such good sports about everything.

So, then I thought, 'Who better to give this book its first review?' I talked to each of the children separately, but they all had basically the same things to say:

"A trip down memory lane."

"Every story is relatable."

"Realistic and personal tales that everyone can relate to."

Thank you, numbers one, two, and three!

Printed in the United States
By Bookmasters